Thor, God of Thunder

Chapter 5
Lesson 78: Murmur Diphthongs *ER, UR,* and *IR*
Lexile® Measure: 580L

ISBN 978-1-62382-036-7

Many years ago during the dark ages, people believed in gods and goddesses. They told stories about them called myths. One of those myths is about Thor. Thor was the son of the Norse gods Odin and Jord. Thor was the god of thunder, lightning, and storms.

Thor was very big and strong. He could hold a thunder bolt in one hand and a big hammer in the other. Thor was so strong he could use his hammer to topple peaks and hills. His job was to protect other gods and people on Earth. He also helped farmers with their crops. If someone was in danger or being hurt, he would hurl his thunder bolt at the evil offender. Thor never shirked his duty to others.

Thor had lots of red hair. He had a big, full beard. He wore a helmet with wings on each side. He also wore a fur cape to protect his shoulders. He had a big, gold magic belt. The belt made him twice as strong.

Thor rode around in a cart pulled by two wild goats. During a battle, his goats looked quite mean when they clenched their teeth. Sometimes lightning bolts would come out from their feet!

His final battle was with Jormungard. He was the Midgard serpent. Thor died from the serpent's bite.

Thor was well-liked by the people in Norway. They even named a day of the week for him. Can you guess which day? It is Thursday, or Thor's day.

The End

Comprehension Questions

1. This passage is about
   a. wild goats.
   b. how the days of the week were named.
   c. a Norse god who used thunder to protect people from harm.

2. Which day of the week is named after Thor?
   a. Sunday.
   b. Thursday.
   c. Hammerday.

3. Which child is in the most *danger*?
   a. a child who is playing with matches
   b. a child who is wearing a seatbelt in a car
   c. a child who is crossing the street with an adult

4. Thor's magic belt made him twice as strong. If he could throw one thunderbolt without the belt, how many could he throw with the belt?

    a. 2

    b. 4

    c. 10

5. What did Thor look like?

    a. He had red hair and a pointed hat.

    b. He had red hair and wore a fur cape.

    c. He had blond hair and wore a shiny cape.

Skill Words

during	danger	shirked
thunder	hurt	fur
hammer	hurl	serpent
farmers	offender	

Most Common Words

a	he	people
about	helped	so
also	him	the
and	his	their
around	if	them
at	in	they
big	is	to
by	it	two
called	liked	use
can	looked	very
come	made	was
could	many	well
day	mean	when
each	named	which
Earth	never	with
even	of	would
for	one	years
from	or	you
had	other	
hand	out	

Challenge Words

believed	wore	guess
hair	shoulders	
beard	magic